What others say about *A Death at Tollgate Creek*:

In Art Elser's new poetry collection, *A Death at Tollgate Creek--Songs of the prairie*, the simple beauties of daily life on the prairie are woven into a tapestry of color, song, scent, heat, and light that invites us to stop and breathe in all the land's sacred and often unseen pleasures. With a near-Buddhist sensibility, Elser shows us "skeins of geese, rising from the lion-colored grass," and Harrier hawks as they "settle, shake out and gently fold/ the feathered gown of long wings." By night, Elser's bell-clear words evoke the "nightly shuffle of the Great Bear," and by evening, "against a turquoise and coral sky," our souls, like his, "want to fly with the cranes." The great stretching distances of wheat, bison, and butterflies that define the landscape of the prairie offers us a precious and rare kind of solitude, one where our minds may "wander back/two-hundred years." --Lori Howe, author of *Cloudshade: Poems of the High Plains*.

Art Elser caught my attention with the first poem, speaking of the "fruitful work of man in nature." Like the "Sounds of a Prairie Morning" of which he writes, his voice reminds us of our "need to listen" for "peace and spiritual renewal." He conjures a saber-toothed cat prowling, herons towing spring north and in his poems, "the living become the dead, /the dead, the living." – Linda M. Hasselstrom has published 15 collections of poetry and nonfiction and conducts writing retreats and online writing consultations from her South Dakota ranch. www.windbreakhouse.com

Looking down while flying over the braided North Platte the poet watches cattle gathering around a stock tank in a windmill's shadow, a tiny tractor plows a field in the half-light, half-dark of dusk, and a thunderhead moves across the high plains dragging grey virga skirts. These all-pervading, energy-carrying images are characteristic of Art Elser's poetry, now collected in "A Death at Tollgate Bridge: Songs of the Prairie," a book where the meadowlark's adagio and the flight speed of the barn swallow over the short-grass prairie draw the reader into a holistic universe, one that is genuine, magical, and at times as visceral as ' the plundered carcass of a pronghorn buck lying in the Autumn grass. – Dan Guenther Author of *The Crooked Truth*.

A Death at Tollgate Creek

Songs of the prairie

Poems by Art Elser
Illustrations by Eileen Roscina

Copyright © 2017 Art Elser
All rights reserved.

Illustrations by Eileen Roscina
Copyright © 2017 Eileen Roscina

No part of this book may be reproduced or transmitted in any form or by any means, electronic or mechanical, including photocopying, recording, or by any information storage and retrieval system without the expressed written permission of the author, except in the case of brief quotations in critical articles and reviews.

ISBN- 978-0-9984554-0-2

WalkerDoodle Press
Denver, CO 80220

*As always to Kate —
my inspiration
and love of my life.*

Acknowledgements

The following poems have been previously published in these journals or anthologies, sometimes slightly changed.

A Bird in the Hand: Harrier Hawks.

Blood, Water, Wind, and Sand: Hope in Early March.

Clark Street Review: A Death at Tollgate Creek.

Distant Horizons: Goose Music.

Emerging Voices: Flyover Country, March Hopelessness, Phoenix Rising from the Marsh.

Encore: Two Weeks After the Vernal Equinox.

Gifts of the Great Spirit: How Sand Lilies Came to Be.

Golden Words, Spotted Horses.

High Plains Register: Elegy for a Barn Owl, The Stranded Barn.

Open Window Review: A Slight Depression, Evening Adagio, The Hunters.

Owl Moon Raptor Center Anthology: At the End of a Warm Fall Day, Golden Eagle.

Serendipity Poets Journal: Aerial Perspective, Winter Sky on the Prairie.

The Weekly Avocet: An Ancient Pilgrimage, Cottonwoods by the Creek, High Plains Thunderstorm, Sounds of a Prairie Morning,

The Avocet: After Many Long Months of Drought, An Almost Full Moon, Bits of Night Hide in the Pines, Brothers Under the Skull, Geese Land in a Small Pond, November Butterfly, The Harbingers, The holy time is quiet as a Nun.

Contents

Acknowledgements iv

Summer 3
- Flyover Country 5
- Sounds of a Prairie Morning 7
- Beautiful Butterfly 9
- The Whisper in the Wind 11
- Brothers Under The Skull 13
- High Plains Thunderstorm 15
- Empty Prairie 17
- Cottonwoods in the Creek 19
- Prairie Morning Challenge 21
- After the Summer Solstice 23

Fall 25
- The holy time is quiet as a Nun 27
- At the End of a Warm Fall Day 29
- After Many Long Months of Drought 31
- Harrier Hawks (after Mary Oliver) 33
- A Death at Tollgate Creek 35
- Phoenix Rising from the Marsh 37
- Geese Land in a Small Pond 39
- Prairie Speedster 41
- Stopping by the Buffalo Herd 43
- And in This Corner, the Challenger 45

Winter 47
- Goose Music 49
- November Butterfly 51
- Bits of Night Hide in the Pines 53
- Evening Adagio 55
- The Hunters 57
- An Almost Full Moon 59
- Golden Eagle 61
- March Hopelessness 63
- A Slight Depression 65
- Winter Sky on the Prairie 67

Spring 69
   Two Weeks After the Vernal Equinox 71
   The Harbingers 73
   Hope in Early March 75
   Squall Line Over Oklahoma 77
   How Sand Lilies Came to Be 79
   The Stranded Barn 81
   Spotted Horses 83
   Elegy for a Barn Owl 85
   Shadow Boxing 87
   An Ancient Pilgrimage 89

About the Author **91**

when I doubt

a loving creator

the meadowlark

Summer

Flyover Country

From thirty thousand feet at night the glow
of city lights from DC to Boston confounds.
If each light represented only one person,
the numbers would astound. Pack too many
rats in a cage and they fight, kill, and eat
each other. How do people thrive, jammed
together like that? Why don't they go crazy?
Violent? Perhaps that's why the evening news
in those cities is so messy.

I'd rather look down at flyover country,
the braided North Platte, emerald green
alfalfa circles, towns with grain elevators
along the railroad, a thin road to an airstrip
two miles out of town, ranches miles apart,
a field half light, half dark, a tractor pulling
the dark thread. Cattle gathered around
a stock tank in a windmill's shadow.
The fruitful work of man in nature.

Sounds of a Prairie Morning

Near the edge of the trail crickets sing for mates.
A meadowlark trills from a mullein stalk.
A grasshopper cruises past, clacking
its way above the grass. A painted lady
flutters by, but her song and wings
are too quiet for human ears.
The low drone of traffic on the highway
a mile away, the sound of human frenzy,
bleeds into the quiet of the prairie.

A pair of Canada geese fly over,
wind whispering in their wings. They call
to make sure the other is still there.
Mourning doves fly up out of the grass,
their wings squeaking softly as they lift.
A goldfinch flies past chirping cheerily.

In a field of thistles by the creek, crickets
are so loud they drown the crunch of boots,
the gliding whistle of airliners sliding
into the Denver airport, and the growl
of feeder planes climbing to Pueblo,

Albuquerque, and Santa Fe.

What a cacophony of song. I prefer
the voices of the two or three crickets
who sing softly here where I sit, and
other prairie sounds that calm me,
the breeze in my ear,
its whisper in the grass,
the melody of a vesper sparrow,
the whiney call of a red-tailed hawk
high in the blue morning.

These sounds of nature quiet my soul,
remind me of my need for solitude,
remind me of my need to listen
for my peace and spiritual renewal.

Beautiful Butterfly

Tiger swallowtail. Wings of gold flashing
in the sun, flitting through the backyard,
looking for nectar, showing your beauty.

Are you nearing the end of your month-long
life? Will you lay your eggs soon
on the leaves of the ash and then die?

Do you, with such beauty, wonder why
your life is so short? Why you can't live out
the summer bringing joy to humans,

enjoying the nectar of backyard flowers?
Each morning as you spread your wings
to let the sun warm your body, do you ask

why you don't have the rich orange
and black and fame of the monarch?
The flight speed of the barn swallow?

Or do you give thanks to the butterfly gods
for the life you have, the sweet nectars
of the garden, your own fragile beauty?

The Whisper in the Wind

A stand of ponderosa pines surround
the barely visible outline of a home that
once stood here. Twenty feet to the west
a depression shows where the family kept
their potatoes, salted meats, root crops,
and ran to hide from summer's twisters.
Bleached fence poles and a snarled roll
of rusted barbed wire marks the garden
where the woman grew vegetables.

The prairie stretches out past infinity
in every direction, a sea of waving grass.
Mountains are tiny bumps to the west.
A cricket and the wind whispering softly
in the pines are the only sounds.

Does it whisper of the family's hope
when they settled here? Or whisper
of their fear when the sand blew in
at every crack in their small home,
buried crops, suffocated their cattle?
Or whisper of despair when they

were forced off the land by drought,
severe winters, the bank?

Or does it just whisper?

Brothers Under The Skull

The snake
      whips
            into a coil
      and rattles.

I freeze,
      intense,
            heart racing,
      breath shallow.

Two primitive, reptilian brains clash
for a second or two—fight or fly?
Then my rational mind returns,
embarrassed by its frenzied retreat.

I laugh, move off a few steps,
beg the snake's pardon, saying
I mean no harm.

Not having man's high-order brain,
the snake stands alert, fierce,
tasting the threat, ready

to attack or be attacked.

Two minutes, danger past,
the snake uncoils and slides off
through the tawny grass.

Its camouflage perfect,
the snake magically
evaporates,
leaving no trace
but the dancing grass.

High Plains Thunderstorm

He watches clouds build over the snowy
spine of mountains, becoming darker
as they grow. One thrusts up taller
than the rest and moves onto the plains,
dragging dark gray virga skirts,
stalking on legs of lightning.

He looks to the dry wheat and hopes the virga
becomes rain. His crops scorched by the sun
three summers now. He'll go bust if a storm
doesn't soon water his fields.

Sky turns green.
Meadowlarks stop singing.
Crows stop flying.
Grasses stop waving.
A great stillness.

The wind comes alive with a sudden gust
from the south, switching quickly west
and back again. Dust swirls from his fields,
hiding the storm until the wind takes it north,

and he can see the swirling darkness.

Shouting over the wind
to his wife, they race
to the root cellar,
close the heavy door.

They cling to each other,
listen to howl and clatter.
It lasts forever . . . and then
a more profound stillness.

They climb from the cellar. The barn roof
has smashed the house, milk house gone,
wheat, hail shredded. They hold each other
and cry.

Empty Prairie

A soft breeze ruffles my gray hair as it whispers through the dry prairie grass. I sit on an east-facing ridge that has scattered artifacts of ancient Indian hunting camps, fire rings, flints, arrow points, pottery shards. My mind wanders back two hundred years. I close my eyes and imagine what Cheyenne hunters must have felt as they saw the bison herds pouring over the ridge to the east, sprinting when they smelled the water in the creek. The Cheyenne knew the bison were coming, first by the dust cloud climbing in the southeast, and then by the thunder of hooves. The ground shook as their hearts must have when they thought of the next morning's hunt. That night they danced, painted their skin and ponies, and prayed to the bison spirit, asking for the meat they needed for their winter-thin families. I open my eyes and see a red-tailed hawk circling over the empty prairie that stretches to every horizon.

Cottonwoods in the Creek

Cottonwoods in the riparian area along
an ephemeral creek, young and old alike
are dying or are dead. Shoots, which showed
promise as new growth, died five years ago
when runoff from new development flooded,
to create a marsh of reeds and cattails.
Ten-year-old trees that would have provided
nesting habitat for red-tails, kestrels, kingbirds,
orioles, and great-horned owls for many years
stand drowned, sad skeletons. Now an intense
two-year drought, brought on by global warming,
stresses century-old trees, limbs and trunks
hollowed and fragile start to fall. The trees,
like Indian tribes in disarray from civilization's
influence, devastated by endemic poverty and
violence, suffer and die from its excesses.

Prairie Morning Challenge

I hike on the short-grass prairie and watch
a pronghorn buck graze calmly seventy yards

away. He lifts his head, looks directly at me,
struts stiff-legged toward me. Thirty yards

out he stops, snorts, lowers his head, sniffs,
paws the ground with a front hoof, squats,

urinates, defecates, and stares again at me,
as if to challenge me to match him.

I laugh, decline the challenge, walk away,
watch him trot off. I assume his challenge
is a blessing from the universe.

After the Summer Solstice

The Sun, ever proud parent, wanting to display
the beauty of Earth, his treasured, spoiled child,
bathes it in his light. Earth thrives in the warmth

of his gaze, bearing flowers, fruit, nurturing
new-born creatures. He wants man to revel
in that plentitude, so each day the light hides

his other children, the planets, Venus, Mars,
Jupiter, Saturn, Earth's Moon, the starry river
of the Milky Way, Orion, and Scorpio's red eye,

the nightly shuffle of the Great Bear, the glorious
infinity of the galaxy-filled Universe. And Earth,
fickle child, soon tires of the light and slowly leans
into winter's darkness and magnificent night sky.

a cricket sings

to an almost-full moon

a harvest song

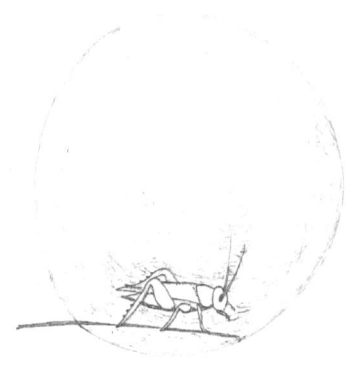

Fall

The holy time is quiet as a Nun

I stride across sage-scented prairie
down a long slope toward the creek.
Crickets chant their love songs, and
the wind sighs softly in the dry grass.
Soon the lights and hum of the city fade
and I stop to sit in the grass and listen
to the prairie quiet. I watch as a full moon
slides upward, silvering a band of high
cirrus clouds, a silk scarf thrown across
the evening sky. The air is soft and warm
and the wind slows as the moon rises
and becomes a complete circle of light.
The crickets begin again to sing a sweet
children's chorus to the night.

My breathing slows as I enter that holy,
peaceful, quiet time. The howl of a lonely
coyote breaks the spell. I laugh. Then,
I howl back, a human voice added
to the chorus of praise.

At the End of a Warm Fall Day

an owl sits in the dusk and softly hoots.
A second owl hoots softly back and joins it

on the branch. They sit together in the light
of the full moon, a middle-aged pair

whose children no longer depend on them.
The owls sit peacefully as if on a swing

on a front porch in Bradbury's Green Town
to enjoy the quiet and each other's company.

After Many Long Months of Drought

the land finally exhales from holding its breath
all summer. Farmers plowed under their crops –
corn and wheat and soybeans – scorched brown
in the hundred degree sun, rains that never came.
Ranchers sold stock when pastures died and hay
became too dear. Hot days have finally given way
to cooler, more seasonal, more comfortable ones.

It's not yet rained, but at least we're not
baking in unrelenting heat. Air that smelled
of wildfires all summer is clearer, mountains
are now visible, sunrises and sunsets softer,
less intense, less vermillion. Flakes of yellow
now lay scattered on the grass under peach
and locust trees, and mountains have put on
their shawls of aspen gold.

Earth breathes life back into her creatures,
blessing them all and everything is glad.

Harrier Hawks (after Mary Oliver)

Regal, swift, silent, they bank and whirl,
brushing the sere grass — elegant
curve of wing, effortless flight.
They glide above the ground, casting,
darting, dancing on the wind.
They search for the slightest
scurrying, scratching, rustle in the dark
shadows of the grass.

Then the up-tilting,
      hovering,
           falling,
                clutching.

Something soft dies.

They settle, shake out and gently fold
the feathered gown of long wings.
Then calmly, they stand with bowed head
as if saying grace. Carefully, with almost
dainty motions, they tear flesh, eat slowly,
at times still, quiescent.

Wings unfold, spread, thrust,
ascend from the grass into graceful,
gliding, searching flight.

In life, small soft creatures dream fearfully
of the sluicing death from the light above.
In death, do they dream
of sun-swept mornings, gliding,
dancing, falling, clutching,

killing?

A Death at Tollgate Creek

The plundered carcass
of a pronghorn buck lies
in the autumn grass.
Hide ripped open.
Ribs, blood red.
Hindquarters gone.
Front legs elegantly crossed.

A trail of matted grass, clumps of white
and tawny fur, where coyotes dragged
and ripped, snarled and ate …
The dead buck, food for their lives.

Two days ago the buck lay whole,
body intact, as if asleep.
Days before, he crossed the creek
and sought a quiet place to die.

The grazing herd
ignored his death,
a natural event,
although he had been

their sire and grandsire.

Wisps of mares-tail clouds soften the sun,
and a warm breeze whispers
in the nodding grass.
To the west, a meadowlark sings.
A quiet scene that mirrors nature:
the living become the dead,
the dead, the living.

Phoenix Rising from the Marsh

The setting sun etches the blue-black
ridge against a turquoise and coral sky.
From the dark in the east comes the calls
of sandhill cranes returning to the marsh.
They become silent, set their wings, glide
to smooth landings, and take a few steps
to stretch graceful legs.

This morning, these same cranes flew
from this marsh, rising like phoenixes
from the ash and mud of the Cretaceous,
the spirits of dinosaurs that died millions
of years ago as that era ended. They lifted
slowly into the dawning sky, like Adam
reaching to the hand of God in the Sistine.

A few weeks earlier, these cranes warbled
high in a prairie morning into the sight
of an old warrior walking there, looking
for peace and solitude. He heard their calls,
like the simple notes of a Beethoven adagio.
His soul wanted to fly with the cranes.

As with emotions he felt in the Sistine Chapel or when he listened to the adagios of Mahler or Beethoven, he could find no words to express the joy he felt in their ancient music.

Geese Land in a Small Pond

Overhead a dozen geese call back and forth
to reach consensus about landing on a prairie pond.

They circle twice to see if danger waits there
in the gathering dusk.

Consensus reached, they start a long slow glide,
but as they near the pond, they shy off,

spooked by something. Honking boisterously,
they flap hard to climb to safety.

Then they turn back, and the leader
starts his glide again.

The others adjust their wings to follow.
Over the pond the flight breaks apart

as each goose picks a spot to swish
to a graceful landing.

Tonight they feed and rest. Tomorrow they continue their journey south.

Prairie Speedster

The pronghorn runs a flying pace
that it can hold for near a mile.
It maintains speed with easy grace
and flowing stride that is its style.

It learned its speed in ice age days
when cheetahs mainly were the foes.
Today bucks use their speedy ways
to race and show off for the does.

With massive lungs and easy stride
this prairie dweller's built to run.
His eyes are keen, he'll quickly hide
from predators and hunter's gun.

Just when you think he's in your fridge,
he's watching from a far off ridge.

Stopping by the Buffalo Herd

A two-thousand pound buffalo bull grazes
near my truck, looking at me with a serene eye
like ones I've seen in pictures of humpback whales.
I'm awed by his massive head and chest. He's lost
most of his winter coat but has shaggy chunks
of dark brown fur hanging as if pieces of his hide
were ripped off. Before wandering to the truck,
he had wallowed playfully on a prairie dog mound,
grunting and letting the sand loosen his winter coat
and dust rid him of flies that cluster on his back.

Two smaller, younger bulls, moved away
as this alpha bull walked down the hill toward
my truck, but cows and calves gather near him.
He suddenly snorts and swiftly pirouettes
as a copper-colored calf accidentally bumps him.
The calf scurries to its mother who is large but
dwarfed by the bull. I look past the cow and calf
and see a curving line of buffalo ambling the half mile
down the ridge toward me, cows, most with a calf
in tow. The line stretches to the top of the ridge.
They kick up dust from prolonged drought.

Memory pulls up a picture of a magnificent herd
of buffalo in an in old-time painting and I imagine
a thousand times the sixty I can see on the hillside.
The immense herd charges over the ridge pursued
by a band of Cheyenne. The swirling dust thunders
with yells of the hunters and bellows and grunts
of the herd. The ground shakes, and I watch in fear
as the fleeing herd races closer. I do not know
where to run, what to do.

Then the bull by my truck grunts, bringing me back
from the ancient herd. He shakes his wooly head
and wanders off toward the creek, past cows and calves
who gather round to see if I've brought food.
I hear their breathing and taste the dust they've raised
and smell the faint aroma of sage they've trampled.

I start the truck and drive away and check the mirror,
half expecting to see a thundering group of buffalo
and Cheyenne warriors pouring down the ridge.

And in This Corner, the Challenger . . .

I come upon a pronghorn buck whose harem
prances nervously, I assume because I'm near.

But the buck isn't looking at me. A second buck,
a challenger, lurks a quarter mile down a slope.

The harem buck takes four stiff-legged steps.

Then he explodes,
an Olympic sprinter
out of the blocks —
a four-hundred-meter race —
full speed in four steps —
graceful flow of menace.

The challenger ducks,
barely escapes,
turns,
faces the buck,
who again charges,
he again dodges,
trots off,

challenge over.

The harem buck canters up the slope, chases down a wandering doe, and they all return to grazing.

early sunbright
cobalt and cold degrees
snowfallglitter

Winter

Goose Music

I walk the faint warmth of a November morning.
A breeze stirs the grass with a soft
hint of sage. The far off honk of geese calls
my eyes to the northeast. Dark lines appear,
skeins of geese, rising from the lion-colored grass.
More and more lines form, stretch
across the sky, touch the horizons.

They fly low, the swish of blue sky
rushing through their wings,
blends with their calls and the sigh
of sere prairie grass.

The cold and snow of a winter storm
squalling in from the north, pushes them south.
Their Vees, though loose and shifting, show
purpose, a journey to warmth and life.

I stand wrapped in morning light …
    watching …
        listening …
            feeling …
the lure of goose music.

November Butterfly

Across a sun-warmed meadow a sulfur
flashes brash yellow wings above sere grass.
Alighting as if to collect pollen the color
of its wings, it balances lightly on a bare stem
that once held a carillon of Bluebells.

The low angle of the sun, its fragile warmth
chilled by each breeze, warns of winter's approach
just behind the mountains. The arching manes
of wispy, cirrus clouds across a turquoise sky
tell of tomorrow's snowbound, flightless death.

Bits of Night Hide in the Pines

Bits of night hide as shadows and cling to dark
branches and trunks as day returns.

Crows, more bits of night in hiding, fly out.
Flocks of red-winged blackbirds,

in the reeds by the marsh, swirl up to remind us
that darkness will soon prevail.

The black bear shuffles down, out of the woods,
to feed and warn us that winter is coming.

After the equinox, these bits slowly come together
to form the long, dark, winter night.

Evening Adagio

Last night, half an hour after sunset,
my dog barked me into the yard to play.
I looked up to see if bats were flying yet.

A few fluttered by in ones and twos.
I watched for a bit before I recognized
the loveliness of the evening light.

The sky shimmered, the luminescent sheen
of blue silk surrounding a Madonna's face,
wrapping her in a vibrant, holy light.

The sky held for a few moments, then
faded into a duller, sadder blue, finally
eclipsed by the gray of coming night.

I was reminded that beauty and sadness
are intertwined. Beauty awakens the soul
with wonder, but sadness must follow.

For the soul cannot bear for long

beauty's exquisite flood of joy.

The Hunters

The setting sun has lost its heat
the hot wind slowly eases
and the sky low in the east

has a spreading magenta stain.
I look from the fluted arrowhead
in my hand across the valley

to a herd of three dozen bison
scattered across tawny hills.
Long ago hunters stood here

looked across the shadowed
valley to a brown river of bison,
raised their voices and spears,

and chanted to the bison spirit
asking for a morning hunt that
would end their winter hunger.

Many years later the hunters
would follow the setting sun
and flowing bison to a valley
where the dark settles early.

An Almost Full Moon

Snow and ice crunch under footfalls.
An almost full moon frees itself
from the winter-bare branches of an old elm
and climbs into the night sky near Jupiter.
Although it's not a frigid night, the moon's light
reflects off the snow covered ground,
pulling the heat from the night and my body.

Why should the night feel so cold?
Perhaps it's the fear our ancestors felt as the fire died
while they sat in the cave and looked into the dark
for the saber-toothed cat who prowled by the light
of an almost full moon.

Golden Eagle

Fierce yellow eyes watch
brown prairie dogs run
across the winter-white field.

Below, sentries stand alert, ready
to bark warnings of death,
diving from above.

Strong yellow talons grip
a snow-cold branch and dream
of warm, yielding flesh, and red,
hot spurts of ebbing life.

March Hopelessness

He awakens to a snow-wind sound,
a soft, hollow whoosh,
like a far-off train hooting
a grade crossing.

He rises and does not see
the hoped-for snow, only
the whipping of leaf-bare branches.

The wind turns suddenly,
howling, tugging, tearing
at the corners of the house.
It batters a gate by the barn.
Rasp .. click . . . . . . bang.
Rasp .. click .. bang.
Then it spins, as if to wrench down
fences, windmills, cottonwoods,
the chaos deepening his depression.

The wheat needs the moisture;
it hasn't snowed in three cold months.

A Slight Depression

This grass-filled hole in the ground
is more a slight depression,
half the size of a grave.
A hundred twenty years ago
a widow and three sons homesteaded here.
Their world was beautiful.
Snow-capped mountains to the west.
An infinite prairie in every other direction.
Just a quarter mile east
a line of cottonwoods marks a small ephemeral creek.
A fading trail meanders down the ridge to the creek,
showing where they hauled water
those first years.
The woman boiled strong coffee
every morning for her family
in that rusted kettle sitting there
half hidden in the grass.
She washed dishes
in that porcelain pan
that's lying upside down
shot full of bullet holes.
Winter evenings,

when work was done,
she sipped dandelion tea
from that shattered china cup.
The two rusted snarls of barbed wire over there
kept their milk cow out of her vegetable garden.
Did drought leave them no garden,
the mule and cattle dead,
unable to "proof" their claim?
Or did an arctic blizzard overwhelm them,
unable to pull water from the frozen well,
unable to retrieve food from the root cellar,
unable to save their animals and themselves?
Where did they go? Why did they go?
Their sod home long melted into the prairie,
leaving only a tea kettle,
a porcelain pan,
a shattered china cup,
a roll of wire,
and a slight depression in the prairie
to mark their passage.

Winter Sky on the Prairie

A brilliant contrail threads
the cobalt fabric of the sky,
twin strands of white wool
pulled by the needle of a jet.
Deep blue stretches from the east
where it wraps around the prairie, west
where it hugs the mountains.

Does the chill air on my skin make
the blue seem so deep? Or does the cold
somehow affect the eyes to make the sky
seem more intense than an azure summer sky?

Whatever the cause, a man could lose
himself in a woman's eyes this blue.

ancient horns
bugle dawning of spring
listen ... cranes

Spring

Two Weeks After the Vernal Equinox

The sun leaps over the prairie horizon
to hear the rhapsody of a returning meadowlark,
a rhapsody that lifts and warbles
through frost-scented air.

Khaki stalks of wheatgrass, buffalograss,
blue grama, and little bluestem, flattened
by heavy winter snows, show green
at their bunched bases.

Winter-thin prairie dogs scout the grass
around their burrows for tender shoots
as they prepare for spring mating
and the birthing of pups.

On toothpick legs, tiny burrowing owls
hunt for burrows that winter has emptied;
the freezing death of prairie dogs
supplies shelter for their chicks.

Antelope does, their bellies swelling
with twin fawns, search the prairie
for newly greened sage, false dandelion,
wild onion, and spreading daisies.

In sandy spaces between clumps
of grass, the hardy, six-pointed
sand lilies and delicate pink phlox
hug the ground with sudden beauty.

The meadowlark continues his rhapsodic
encouragement to arriving robins,
his ecstasy giving voice
to the promise of nature's renewal.

The Harbingers

The pond, long hostaged by ice,
reflects the early dawn.
A single Heron is etched
in the chill, brittle light.

He would have struggled there
last week, slender legs,
stiletto bill no match
for the pond's icy crust.

The bird's tall, liquid shape
foretells the quickening thrust
of Lupine and Pasque Flowers,
soon to grace the earth.

Overhead last night, two Herons
rowed north, arrow straight, on strong,
blue wings. Silent harbingers,
towing spring behind.

Hope in Early March

The road washboards to the horizon
where an eternity away the arid land
meets a sterile blue sky and is pinned there
by barbed wire, dirty snow, and tumbleweeds.
Power lines measure the road.
In spring hawks, meadowlarks, and doves,
will perch on them, but now they are bare.
A kestrel dives for food and climbs,
talons empty. A few cows appear,
their scattered dearth mirroring
abandoned ranches, trailer homes,
and rusting pickup trucks.

A few dozen antelope, spread over miles,
search the prairie for food with such intensity
they don't look up as passing cars
trail rooster tails of dust.

In the distance, a shape appears in the corner
of two fence lines, a black angus cow.
She's just given birth, the blood-red placenta
still hanging. Nearby a teetering calf,

black fur wet from birth and tongue,

falls, struggles back up, finds

its mother's teat, and sucks lustily,

oblivious to winter's desolation.

Squall Line Over Oklahoma

I'm flying from Alexandria, Louisiana,
to Oklahoma City. The night sky ahead
has a strange glow as if I'm approaching
a large city. But I am miles from any.

Soon, thunderstorms fill the horizon,
from Texas to Kansas. Powerful energy fills
the sky with stuttering sheets of lightning
and brilliant flashes that strike the ground.

Cloud tops are forty thousand feet above,
and my small plane would fail to climb
even half that high. It looks as if I'll have
to turn around and wait out the storms.

But the sky is so beautiful, miles of glowing
cumulus against a black sky. I fly parallel
to them to enjoy their beauty with the faint hope
that I'll find a way through. I fly on, amazed.

Then a hole appears. I fly between two
huge, flickering clouds and head for home.
I watch the storms until I turn to land,
stunned by the beauty of this night.

How Sand Lilies Came to Be

This morning I asked wise-one-who-heals
where the sand lilies came from.
They are the first flowers each spring
and always grow in bare spots where
the grass hasn't started to turn green.
Their six white petals, the color of snow
and golden center, the color of the sun,
seem so fragile and beautiful against
the cold, the sere grass, and brown earth.
When I see them my heart is glad.
He said that long ago great herds
of Hotoa'e roamed the land
and the people hunted them
for food and skins and other
things needed for daily life.
Then the white man drove away
the herds and the people suffered.
No more meat to feed their families.
No more skins for tents and clothes.
No more bladders to boil food in.
No more scrotums to make sacred rattles.
No more horns to make medicine spoons.

The people were desperate and they asked
the holy men to pray to the spirit of Hotoa'e.
Hotoa'e heard their lament and answered them.
He said that the great herds had gone
under the ground but some day they would return.
As a sign of his promise to the people,
Hotoa'e turned their tears into the sand lily.
Where their tears fell the sand lily now blooms
to remind them that the great herds
will some day come back.

The Stranded Barn

The barn, brought low by time and snow,
has settled like a sailing ship stranded
on a bar. Once it sheltered horses, cows,
and sheep from blizzards, hail, and heat,
but now a pile of gray warped boards
in land reclaimed by sere prairie grass.

Only traces remain of the family who
lived here, a faint trail through the grass
that leads to cottonwoods by the creek--
a wife, three children buried there—
a gray concrete outline is all that tells
that once they lived and loved and hoped.

Two pregnant mule deer watch me
from the trees. They and the sand lilies
at my feet the only vestiges of hope.

Spotted Horses

> *Scientists studying DNA to discover the colors of horses painted on cave walls 25 to 30 thousand years ago found that "... there were really only these three color patterns — spotted or dappled; blackish ones; and brown ones ...."*

The leggy Appaloosa colt first walks

then trots a lazy path around his dam.

He gallops off through tawny prairie grass

and finally finishes his head-long charge

to nuzzle lovingly his mother's face.

They're two white horses kissed with leopard spots

who seem like mirror images or else

that they have floated off the walls of caves

in France to drop into this sun-blessed field.

The scientists who study DNA

have found those leopard spots have been around

for thirty thousand years; they've found a gene

that inks those spots. Do you suppose they'll find

that pony's genes for spirit, grace, and joy?

Elegy for a Barn Owl

I saw you a quarter mile away, a motionless
dark cruciform, hanging from the top wire
of a fence. You made a last second change
to your slashing dive to catch an unsuspecting
mouse, and caught that metal barb instead.

How long did you struggle there unable
to free yourself, unwilling to die? Did you
hiss and snap your terrible hooked beak
and flash your deadly talons at the coyotes
who would have killed, ended your pain?

When did life leave your fierce eyes?
When did peace finally release you?

Shadow Boxing

His thin body
and gangly legs,
pounce
and spring
and paw
and dance
like a young man
shadow boxing at the Y.

The coyote pup plays
on a prairie ridge line,
alert, scanning, sniffing,
searching for fun or food.

The young boxer trains
for rounds of 3-minutes,
the coyote pup
for survival.

He's boxing real shadows.

An Ancient Pilgrimage

A flock of sandhill cranes takes flight
and trills their haunting primal song.
They start to rise from earth as if
they've heard some loud ancestral call.

And as they pass they call to coax
the nearby cranes to come with them.
Then soon the air is filled with wings
to start their ancient pilgrimage.

They find a stream of rising air,
and set their wings to soar and climb.
The vortex of the rising birds
pulls others from the nearby fields.

The flock turns north to search for mates
and breed a thousand miles away.

About the Author

Art Elser retired after 20 years as an Air Force pilot and 30 as a technical writer. He has a PhD in English and taught writing for over 30 years. His poetry been published in *Voicings from the High Country*, *Owen Wister Review*, *High Plains Register*, *Harp Strings Poetry Journal*, *Science Poetry*, *The Avocet*, *Open Windows Review*, and *A Bird in the Hand: Risk and Flight*. His chapbook, *We Leave the Safety of the Sea*, received the Colorado Authors' League Poetry award for 2014.

He lives in Denver with Kathy, his wife of 35 years and their dog, Walker.

www.ingramcontent.com/pod-product-compliance
Lightning Source LLC
Chambersburg PA
CBHW021134300426
44113CB00006B/419